WHEN YOU WERE
INSIDE MOMMY

by JOANNA COLE
illustrated by MAXIE CHAMBLISS

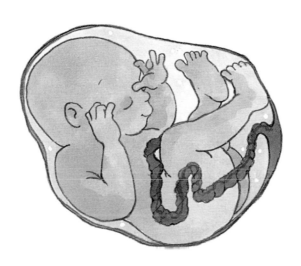

HarperCollinsPublishers

Once you were inside your mommy.
Did you know that?
It's true!

Before you were born, you lived
in a special place in Mommy's body
called the uterus, or womb.

It's a safe, warm place where babies can grow.

In the beginning you were just one tiny cell.
Half of the cell came from your mommy,

and the other half came from your daddy.
That cell was smaller than this dot! .

You started growing right away.
Soon you looked like this.

Then like this.

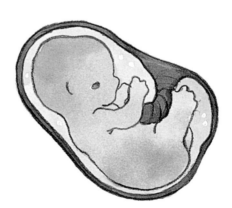

And this.

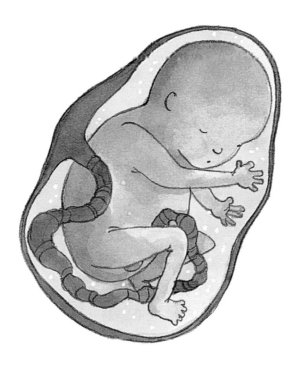

You were much more than a dot now!
You had eyes and a nose and a mouth.
You had hands and feet and fingers
and toes.

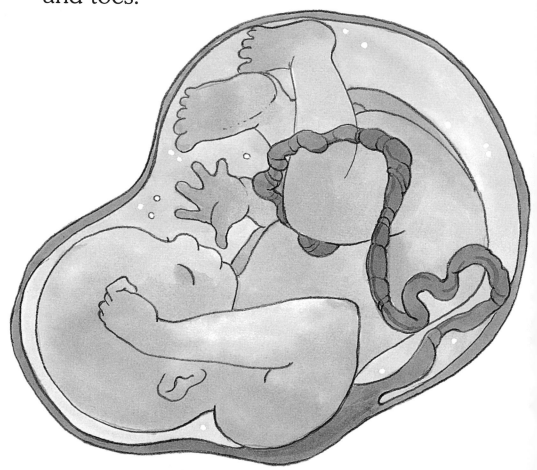

Mommy's belly had to stretch *way* out to make room for you.

Mommy and Daddy went to the doctor.
The doctor helped them listen.
Do you know what they heard?
"Beat, beat, beat, beat. . . ."
It was the sound of
your little heart beating!

Before you were born, you didn't eat
or drink or breathe the way you do now.

Food and air came from Mommy's body
through a long tube called the umbilical cord.
All that good food helped you
grow and grow and grow.

You were in the womb for about nine months. Then Mommy and Daddy knew you would be born any day.

Your crib was all set up.
You had a big stack of diapers,
a cute teddy bear,
and a nice warm baby blanket.
Everything was ready.

Now all Daddy and Mommy had to do was wait.

They waited . . .

and waited . . .

and waited. . . .

Then one day it happened.
Mommy felt the muscles of her
womb squeezing.
You were starting to be born!

At the hospital Mommy pushed you out through a special opening in her body that can stretch wide to let a baby through.

Daddy and Mommy were so happy.
"Hello, little baby," they said.
"We love you!"

A nurse washed you off and put on
a diaper, a shirt, and a little hat to keep
you warm.

You drank milk from Mommy's breasts
or from a bottle.
Soon you were fast asleep.

After you were born, you kept growing.

Just look how big you are now!
Mommy and Daddy are proud of you.

No matter how big you grow, isn't it fun to know that you were once inside Mommy!

A Note to Parents

Answering Children's Questions about Birth

It's Natural
All children wonder where they come from. It's natural for them to ask. When you answer questions in an affectionate, accepting way, you show that you approve of your child and his or her natural curiosity.

Clear Up Confusion
Young children often have misunderstandings about birth. Sometimes their confusion can cause worries. Before answering, ask, "What do *you* think?" By finding out what your child understands, you can give a more helpful answer.

Keep It Short and Simple
It's best to give only the information a child seems to want at the time. Too much information all at once may be overwhelming. Many short talks are better than one big one.

Expect Repeat Questions
Young children will sometimes forget what they have been told. In addition, the same

information has more meaning at later stages of their development. Expect to answer questions more than once.

Admit You Don't Know
No one knows everything, and sometimes a question stumps a parent. When you don't know, say you'll find out—and keep your promise.

Be Available to Talk
Tell your child that you always welcome questions. Open the door by saying, "Often children have questions about how they were born. If you have one, I'll be glad to talk about it."

Facts and Feelings
The facts about birth cannot be separated from a child's feelings. Children want to hear the story of their own birth because it assures them that they are loved and tells them how much they have grown. Tell the story in a loving way.

It's a Happy Subject!
Take your child's questions seriously, of course, but why should the discussion have a serious, instructional tone? Keep it light and warm.

Library of Congress Cataloging-in-Publication Data
Cole, Joanna.
    When you were inside Mommy / by Joanna Cole ; illustrated by Maxie Chambliss.
       p.   cm.
    ISBN 0-688-17043-9
    1. Pregnancy—Juvenile literature.   2. Childbirth—Juvenile literature.   [1. Pregnancy.
2. Birth.]   I. Chambliss, Maxie, ill.   II. Title.
    RG525.5.C643   2001   00-040890
612.6'3—dc21   CIP
                                                                                                         AC

22 SCP 20 19 18 17 16 15 14
❖